Love & Depression

Morgan Dale

While every precaution has been taken in the preparation of this book, the publisher assumes no responsibility for errors or omissions, or for damages resulting from the use of the information contained herein.

Love & Depression

First edition, February 29, 2024.

Written by Morgan Dale.

i can't pluck a string
to save my life
but i can hum a chord or two

tell me the meaning
of your silly words
before i get bored of you

express the feelings
that i know you have
in need of a shorter fuse

this is exactly
what you want it to be
let them report the news

paint them the landscape
that they want to see
i can distort their views

frigid air takes me back
to the place i stand
i'll sing a warmer tune

transition from audience
to silent eyes
that's the performer's cue

- a chord or two

our conversations
bring about reinvigoration
i'm staring up at the constellations
constantly waiting for things to change

i don't have the time for the planets
to realign and rearrange
into an opportunity

for opulence and unity

i realize that the
offer isn't truthfully extended

i'd be pretending if i said
i don't want you to end it

no matter the outcome,
i'm glad to have befriended

glass panes that frame
elation, i stand behind it

the art's timeless,

there isn't a point to refine this
the part that i can't shake
is how hard it's been not to mind it

seldom in need of reminding

i'm searching for something
i may never wind-up finding

- opulence and unity

i can hear the lake
calling my name

walking through the lilies
until i find peace

the water's just fine,
you should jump in

your endeavor's dated
by the timepiece

looking to the fire
and the ashes

nature shows that
everything will cease

the catch is that
you'll never know the timeline

maybe this is really
what the thrill seeks

\-   timepiece

endless shifts move rifts
in the opposite direction

do dismiss true quips
with requisite reflection

who is it who flips
tales of another perspective?

   - requisite

she had those eyes

they could lasso the moon

voicemail artifacts
your voice, begins to decay
and wash away

gave feelings of flight

floating with the balloons

magnetic attraction
the choice, for us to stay
has gone astray

soft skin to the touch

sliding down the dunes

slipping through the cracks
the fix, doesn't need delay
buried under the clay

heaven-sent oasis

our romantic lagoon

there's no time to react
i froze, what it conveyed
more than i can say

\- voicemail artifacts

down in the pits, i'm mining
for something i'm never finding
they call it the perfect timing
for the shining to occur

so the whining that you heard
is intertwining with the birds
when rewinding all the words
there's no defining the absurd

it's never odd or even
when you're trying to paint the picture

it's hard to reach completion
when you know you ain't the pitcher

it's tough to change the season
when you can't adjust the fixture

there's balance to this life
we're all looking for the mixture

- down in the pits

houston
i'm losing transmission

around me are the stars
and i know they hear me wishing
her voice is the sound
that i know i've been missing
the silence of space
is all that i can listen to

i don't think i'm getting through
looking down on earth
is my only view

my journey has been
to get to you

but lately, things have changed
and that's no longer true

my course is now set
and i know it can't move

i'll be thinking of you

it's cold out here

i don't crack a smile
    i only shed a tear

            i don't feel warmth
            i only feel fear

of not returning home
  or ever coming near

i see on the horizon
things i've never seen
they tell me that it's true
what's shining from the beam

            when stars glisten
        i see through the sheen
    that where i've been going
        is where i want to be

i know i'm going home

i know i'll be there soon

happiness is buried
under layers of the gloom
it comes in waves
like the cycle of the moon
the sun is now setting
on this drawn-out tune

i know i'm in reach

i can see the peak

as gravity weighs
my thoughts can seem bleak
but i found a way
to see things when i sleep
they show me how to climb
when i'm in too deep

i thrust the ignition

i know i found a way

my course is set to home
and i'm landing in a day
when i reach earth
i open up the bay
to see i missed the chance
for the things i couldn't say

i watch you take off

i watch you disappear

i gaze upon the stars
their message isn't clear
so i look to my dreams
so i can hold you near
these are the memories
that i share with you, my dear

- takeoff

i don't have a purpose
feel tired, detached, worthless
rather stay in bed than
play a part in the circus

balancing on the tightrope
makes me feel nervous

onlookers stare while they
remain on the surface

giving hot takes that
come straight from the furnace

when i fall,
surges of nurses
will attempt to reverse
nature's urges

- balancing act

you were the one
  i couldn't entertain

rainy days
felt like a hurricane

we live landlocked
    so it seems insane

suppose we'll follow
the weather vane

twisting and turning

those bridges are burning

i know that you're yearning

for some way out

from what i'm discerning

there's no overturning

the things you're concerning

you'll figure it out

as far as the crow flies
 go and spread your lies
  can't look me in my eyes

i have no doubt

sad as the blue skies
and i bet that time flies
when even the sun cries

pray for a drought

- weather vane

i find nostalgia
staring at my ceiling fan

it hasn't moved
in a couple of years

i can't seem to turn it on
and the screws are stripped

all the bulbs have burnt out
so it's losing its purpose

i find that sometimes
i can feel the ceiling fan

staring back at me
though intent is never clear

i didn't check the breaker
to see if it had tripped

but it's getting late
so maybe it's not worth the hassle

- ceiling fan

i can see the rose buds
all she does is roll drugs
while i sip on cold suds
she prays he shoots duds

i can see the willow cry
deep inside she often hides
the sorrow, so tomorrow
repeating lows and highs

i can see the tides shift
hanging off the high cliff
below you'll find the rift
with the people that i miss

i can see the sunset
time for her to undress
wash away with numb sex
are we having fun yet?

i can see the sky glow
will she ever find home?
taken from the undertow
wonderful, the things that i know

the things that i know

i can hear the waves crash
how long will this train last?
stops that we have blown past
i've paid out no cash

i can hear the birds hum
lips where the words come
moments like these
indeed, are worth some

i can hear the oak creek
this is where the folks meet
images in my sleep
of stories you never told me

i can hear the breeze stop
told what i believe not
to be true; i knew
where the maple leaves drop

i can hear the river flow
frozen during winter snow
time for me to let her go
wonderful, the things that i know

the things that i know

- yew

the reclusive
late-night soliloquy

      sharing his thoughts
but wonders who is he

upon reflection,
what do you see?

      someone you feel
that you want to be?

perhaps the question
has been haunting me

    - soliloquy

a plateau,
vast plains
i'm flat-footed

tar pits,
ghast remains
i know i shouldn't

indulge the spirits
that lurk in the shadows

there's murk in the shallows,
but hidden treasures
can lead a search
to the gallows

tailor the script towards
a sailor who can't a grip
of the ripcord, seeing the ship torn,
by devilish lips sworn to secrecy,
from the surface of the sea

the map has been lost to piracy,
but the legacy stakes a claim,
embossed quietly

like a scar that's hard to see
or a star that's too far to gleam

- hidden treasures

and i try my best,
give everything that
i have to offer

would they feel the same
if i wasn't successful
and did not prosper?

all these golden ideas
may just turn into some
worthless copper

rather know where i stand
and live my life as a
lonely pauper

- prosper

my head's under water
    i'm trying to keep up with my daughter
she keeps hiding these secrets
    that's something that i never taught her

    to tell the truth that's a lie
i'll do whatever to disguise
    my impending demise
but baby please recognize

that you and i are far more similar
than you would expect

        we're both growing by the minute
        and it's hard to detect

    i haven't had a chance to sleep
    because i'm drowning in debt

        so i drink away my sorrows
            and i sink to the depths

there i notice my son
and he gives me a wave
but i know i'm the one
he wouldn't choose to save

he'd rather cruise away
he's battered, bruised, and frayed
he's shattered, who's to say
he wouldn't lose his way

i couldn't prove dismay
has made me make mistakes
i maybe take the cake
my babies hate to ache

you don't know how hard my life is

you'll never know these sacrifices

you don't know the strength of my vices

someday you'll connect the slices

- mama's misery

her vast ocean

of emotions

swells with tears

from fears

of hearing

the end is nearing

peering into the mind

i find that time

has left us

lost at sea

- ocean

there lies a colorful plain
  filled with beautiful flowers
      as far as the eye
        can see

    between the red carnations
      and black roses,
        a dark stream
      begins to flow

    as the soft trickle
  turns into a furious rapid,
        the ground starts
              to erode

        it cuts deep into the soil
          and tears away
            the delicate life
                that lives above

quickly, a dam is constructed
to prevent further damage
to the defenseless,
fragile field

the ground acquires a thirst,
and the flowers
begin to wilt
and decay

toward the desert
or the ocean,
where am i
to go?

- thirst

i walk through the desert
and measure the pleasure
that's derived from those surprised
to be alive today telling their tales

tearful eyes and fearful lives
        are dreadful tales that sound like i
                though i can't lie that i know why
                        their thoughts are truly mine

gloomy tombs scatter the dunes
        and prove that most
accept their fate and dissipate
        until they're a ghost
    glasses filled with sadness
just happens to be the perfect toast
    matches thrown that gaslit
the masses who never made it home

- desert

i'm barely caring
i'm barely sharing

how much i may be drinking
what i may be thinking

of what i could be doing
or what i may be viewing

i'm peering through the glass
i'm moving through the grass

i notice things undone
i know my time will come

i'm just trying to breathe
i'm just trying to ease

all the things i know
all the things that grow

to be far too large
to be far too big

to know that i am a cow
and that you are a pig

to have a head of hair
and to choose the wig

     to say you're done at last
     and then take the gig

to say you're done at last
and then take the swig

     if i could
     bring you back

       i would

      you know that

- what i may be viewing

the pill is hard to swallow
but you should let it in
it's medicine

wash it down with your sorrow
you'll feel better then
it's medicine

swig the flask till it's hollow
then repeat again
it's medicine

hope you live to see tomorrow
i pray it's menacing
it's medicine

- blake's bitterness

she got her name
  from an old band

she doesn't know
what she could command

perspective she lacks,
but would she understand

deserving of more
from what you call your man

the world is something
that you oughta have

but you share doubts
while we share a glass

expecting nothing
from your other half

has left you wondering
if you'll last

you say he's young
in time you'll see him grow

as years go by
you look at what you sow

a desolate field
there's nothing to show

my thoughts are racing
then i hear you go

i'm inside the riptide
and that's how i get by

i got to let things slide
and that's how i live life

know what i see?

a catch in the big sea
a catch that you would be
a man on one knee

she got her name
from an old band

not quite sure
how she withstands

a puzzle to solve
in the motherland

lucky for her
she's got the upper hand

the moon is something
that you oughta see

no need to look
for an odyssey

a journey to space
or heading out to sea

you'll know where it is
ain't need it out of me

a leap of faith
might be the only way

because you'll look back
on another day

asking the question,
why did i stay?

before she jumps
i know i heard her say

i'm inside the riptide
and that's how i get by

i got to let things slide
and that's how i live life

know what i see?

a catch in the big sea
a catch that you would be
a man on one knee

- riptide

i walk through the forest
explore it, adore the various colors
warily wander and wonder
if more is to be uncovered

under the sticks, leaves, and rocks
i'd search all the spots
for subtle reminders
more rubble
rebuttal with,
i will find her

speaking to an old timer
who reminisces on those he misses
he wishes he could've listened
to his past wishes but lives with
the fact that he dismisses
his misses as someone who isn't
the person he'd prefer to live with

cabin in the woods
is his loneliest endeavor
whether or not it's spacious
he's faced with the thought
that will never be forgot
was the chance wasted?

- the forest

progression
lately feeling like regression
i don't know why i've been stressing
all my goals have been expected
all my thoughts have been infected
i don't know why i've accepted
always feeling like i'm left with

a choice to throw it
all away

her complexion
matches my obsession

her discretion
mirrors my reflection

some lessons
time i've always been investing
find that i can't stop dissecting

moments,

then second-guessing
silence is the secret blessing
dreaming of a final resting
thinking if it's worth contesting

a choice to throw it
all away

her complexion
matches my obsession

her discretion
mirrors my reflection

- complexion

i'd revel in your death
but i don't want to

i wish i felt love
like when i met you

if only there were things
i could undo

i'd ruin your sunshine
and make your days blue

the source of my strength
is now my weakness

i hope your pain
will cut the deepest

fade away on mars
while i'm on venus

i know your nights
will all be sleepless

- haley's hatred

light blue haze
weighs down the morning mood
blur ways of perturbed days
an uneasy malaise

yellow beams blind and mellow
i am but the chartreuse fellow
pale the skin, with sunken eyes
frail begins to come alive

maroon headaches
until noon, then eventually dissipate
no wonder i slumber
not an obligation to be late

deep blues
return like
they did before

i implore the red
to dismiss
it to the door

purple compromises
with violence
and silences
the worries

colors are distorted
mixed with sharpness
contorted is he
who proceeds
to venture
deep into the darkness
the cycle begins
to spin again
as he wakes
and feels
so heartless

\-   prison's prism

i can see it in sight
i know i've almost made it

suppose my thoughts and feelings
were probably overstated

i take a deep breathe in
you know how long i've waited

      but then this hole i've left
        is truly situated

inside a marvelous crater
that's appearing outdated

although the challenge is greater,
i act as if i'm elated

because i know the creator
and myself are related

      i opt to deal with it later
      until i'm more elevated

embark upon the journey
my systems are regulated

i act as if my choices
are simply unrelated

to the hill i climb
and the decisions i've hated

i know i'd do it again
i feel like i'm obligated

it's the moment at last
the same one i have awaited

i've thought about it for ages
to one day be liberated

and then my body goes numb
when i see where i am located

i'm looking off at a planet
from where i am isolated

- marvelous crater

i'd rather not,
but if you insist

the slit on her wrist
is a glimpse of innocence

relive the incident
with stark vividness
giving off simpleness
when i try synthesis

young prince nicholas,
his imminence

the lack of emotion
was brought up by his fickleness

blood dripping down
to the start of the impetus

picture of the noble
was clouded by the wickedness

soon found vigilance
then dissonance

echoes through the cranium
began seeming limitless

nervous brittleness
made thinking villainous

there's no equivalence
to how she felt when
spilling this

his omnipotence
wasn't too chivalrous
shiver from the choices
that are now seeming
frivolous

his ambivalence
looked as though meticulous

likely that his impotence
cemented her as
infamous

and i would be remiss
if i didn't mention
how much
i miss
you

- young prince nicholas

and i'll keep running
you know i will

i've made it this far
i haven't moved an inch

i haven't felt a thing
they say it's part of the thrill

so then i take my aim
i know i'm shooting to kill

legend says he's gone
he's now the king of the hill

it's a matter of moments
before he thinks he's ill
alone atop the mountain
with only time to fill
it's only time that heals

i've been ignoring how i feel
i feel like things aren't real
i need some time to deal

with who i wanted to be

with what i wanted to say

with where i wanted to go

with how i'm feeling today

and what i do not know

- king of the hill

might seem to expect
i know what i'm doing
but i assure that i don't

write me a text
so when it comes to replies
i'm sure that i won't

likely an expense
that i'll have to keep feeding
until i'm broke

might see what's next
and you know that you'll
have to speak with my folks

\-   overdose

lately, i've been
spending my time alone
with no one to reach
a waste of a phone

lately, i've been
having fun in the unknown
waking from dreams
a place to call home

i have not a clue
when my preference will change
i prefer the landscapes
i can rearrange

motions through the day
start to seem real strange
lately, waking up feels
like a worthless exchange

- landscapes

we'd drive down main street
stop at the store

luggage repair
never heard of that before

ignoring our cares
playing cards on
the floor

hell of a bet
the odds are twenty
to one

the year went by
i guess twenty was fun

drugs are a place
where the money will run

you try to catch up
but you lose the pace

the image is clear
but i lose your face

memories are based
on how you choose to taste

sprinkle in the time
that i refuse to waste

lying through the lips
that i used to kiss

sounds like a song
that is hard to miss

everyone insists
that you cover your ears

i choose to play along
as to silence the fears

- lose the pace

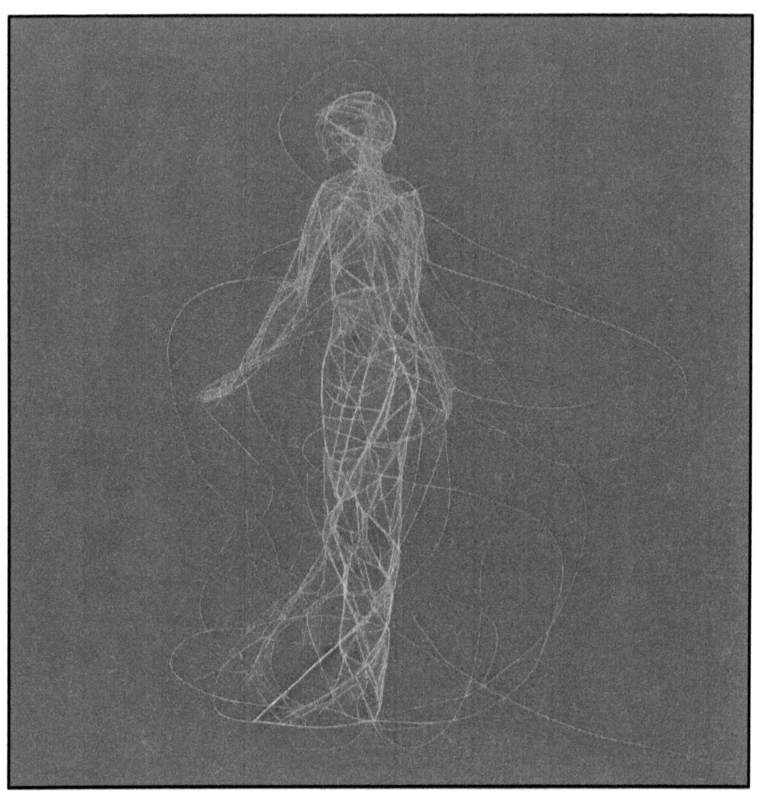

you don't know how often
that i search
through car windows,
on the sidewalks,
near all the places
you used to be

you don't know how often
that i wish
our stories were different,
on stars that never come,
you were the person
you used to be

you don't know how often
that i lie
to people who care,
about how i feel,
and say i don't miss who
you used to be

- always

and i'm all ears
please do tell

i'd like to make things clear
and state that i'm not well
i'd like to share my story
to show how far i fell

but have you considered
all the cars you sell?

wheeling and dealing,
now feeling that you ain't right?
squealing and reeling,
now stealing all the limelight?

i used to be appealing
and i used to shine bright
it seems to be revealing
that concealing all my plight
has stunted most my healing
now i'm pealing in the light
i used to want to ceiling
now i'm dealing with the height

this has been appealing
but i think it just might
fade into obscurity,
vanish to the night
displaying merely purity,
leave damage from the sight
you'll need some security
you're famished from the flight

- please do tell

memories found buried
under the rat piss and filth

much like the gold
that is lost in the silt
or the rose that's seen
only after it begins
to wilt

this is what negligence
has chosen to be built

-   in the silt

i'm floating on the seaside
conducting on the tracks
mother is a free guide
one duckling made it back
my motive is an onus
so, no clucking when i crack
i'm hoping no one notices
when i'm plucked into a quack

waving at passersby
        who look to give a lift
saving the azure tide
        from crooks who live adrift
braving the mastermind
        who took to steering skiffs

he lived to tell the tale, but
you're hooked to hearing
        myths

i've suspended comprehension
you intended nothing rude

but the tension of attention
has descended on the crew

spraying all the diesel
and the evil until it takes
pray it won't be lethal
though i'm gleeful in the wake

it's peaceful on the surface
but you feel the undertow
lose my train of thought
when i wonder where i'll go
the easel and the canvas
always going toe to toe
i'm betting on the struggle
while they're trading blow for blow

at high noon, the typhoon
will make waves
i'll try to sing my tune,
a mayday
then find who's a tycoon
and trade days
but might soon find my mood's
the same way

the smoke cascades
over broke past days
with no hope to tote
my last play was to choke
and blast away

he's coaxed with cash today
but knows the rations may
lead to thrashing and that happens
to be the action that got traction

he soaks into his grave
he's hopeless, but he's brave

you're joking; he's just insane

you've broken the painted pane
you've opened the tainted scares
there's nothing he could attain
to live up to what you are
he's burning up in the stars

the bloke's a castaway
what folks will laugh and say

we're stoked the forecast
is at last infinite grey

provoke, although it may
they spoke off beaujolais
awoke to find the bottle
was clouked as cabernet

- painted pane

off to st. pete's
with pictures, that's the keepsake
hoist the sail
mother told me to keep safe
one day journey
spent looking towards deep space
coconut rum, tropical tobacco
sweet taste
my compass never let me down
that's why i greet faith
with open-armed optimism
often each day
but when i reached land
that belief saw decay
after viewing the remains

what remained?

a beach grave

off to st. mia's
hitting patches of some rough waves
battering the ship
i'm in for a few tough days
worth the torment
the island couldn't get enough praise
bunch of those bungalows
improved indigenous ways
compass stopped functioning
but i could see the sun glaze
over the potential
buried by a robust blaze
on the shore, i made contact
with a numb gaze
eyes told the story
of a stardust craze

off to st. carmen's
i'm drunk off the hearsay
slow from the tears
and the holes in the rear bay
lo and behold
spent nearly a year astray
remember seeing life
memory was clear as day

short-lived
soon i was caught in dismay
how could beauty turn sour
in every which way?

now i know
that'll have to disengage
avoid the downfall
and the widespread plague

these are islands
but these are people
i've been trying
to keep it simple
know i'm lying
through these dimples
though i'm crying
i say that it'll

-   islands

i moved a stone,
underneath stood a toad

i heard a croak,
unbelieving of its tone

it rang true
to what i used to
hear at home

the same view
as if he was
my only clone

then i spotted another
he was likely a friend

he came, and he went
before i could apprehend

he must've assumed
i was gifting an end

i'm merely an oracle
shifting the trend

i know this story
like the back of my hand

seeking advice
from the preaching man

he charted a course
that has me reaching land

before i'm able to walk
on the beach's sand

so i choose to sail
by the whims of the wind

i'm sharing my story
by the hymns that i've tinned

my eyes feel tired
and i begin to look thin

but nothing compares
to the grimness within

- whims of the wind

these are the hours during which
belligerence ricochets off the walls,
crawls beneath closed doors,
and suffocates the space.

these are the moments
that disappear from your memory
to calm the turbulent waters
from wreaking havoc upon the ship.

on occasion they surface
as a reminder to the castaway
that what can be forgotten
can never be changed.

the harbor will show you
the turmoil endured
from journeys that lasted
well past their provisions.

missing are the boats
that truly suffered the most
for they are the ones
that never felt
the calm.

- the missing boats

over the hills
i imagine better scenes

reaching the apex
isn't what i dreamed

so my beautiful state
or so it seems

is really me lost
in the reverie

down in the valley
i find other means

to lift myself
above the evergreens

so my limelight
though as it gleams

is propped up by
a devilish fiend

near the clouds
my vision's so keen

before the problems
were all unseen

although it's peaceful
what you don't see

is all the others
behind the smoke screen

- above the evergreens

he quivers, he's frozen
beginner has chosen
a sinner who's loathing
over the past
and what once was

the thinner he's growing
the quicker he's knowing
it's bitter, it's going
far too fast
for what once was

i don't know
when my life
will change

but i hope it will,
and i hope it's soon

i don't know
how things
got this bad

but i hope someday
i'll sing a different tune

the days blend together
and my memories fade

hanging by a tether
and the fabric is frayed

acting like i'm strong
but i'm truly afraid

of what could go wrong
if i choose to stay

- what once was

at the top of the citadel
heights where the pigeons fell
or pushed, though i wish them well
no choice if you couldn't tell
feelings that i wouldn't quell
places that i shouldn't dwell
emotions that begin to swell
no buying stories that i sell

picking up new clientele
hiring some personnel
mindset seeming parallel
now we out here raising hell
hungry souls, dinner bells
winding up in prison cells
after sending bullet shells
towards those carousels

- robert's rage

down by the river
here you'll find the sinners,
   or so it's said
finding those swimmers
   on the riverbed

where the hopes and dreams
            are ever dead
         and it almost seems
            that the river bled

   down by the river
no one is a winner,
   or so it's said
air is getting thinner
   from the bitter dread

where the note he leaves
      is but a thread
      of what he means
            by the river red

   - the red river

mina,
now's not a good time to talk
i haven't found my place

you haven't shown your heart
can't you see it's a waste
to spend all your energy
lost in space?

i'd rather float away
than tether myself
to an unknown fate

how about we set a date
and watch the hands tick by
to see if you can find
where you want to reside

what if i show up late?
how might the crowd respond?

a fish on dry land
always gets to the pond

or dies on its way

tell me the difference
to how you currently feel

- watch the hands tick by

the
never-ending
staircase
spiraling
down below
bellows from
the abyss
and rioting
flames
that glow
wishing
they could
ascend
but deeper
they
may go

cracked marble ledges
on the surface lay snow
found to be ashes
of people you don't know
how can i come back
when i've descended
this low?

- the never-ending staircase

my world has shattered
i'm lost in oblivion
to know that i will never
be able to see you again

i wish i could forget
and let you be free

to remember all the ways
that we used to be

i'm aching with sorrow
more than you know
but i'll always love you
regardless of where you go

everything is different
between you and me

but i'm hoping it will change
we'll just have to see

- oblivion

saloons in amarillo
blue moons and amaretto
liqueurs, i am a little
tipsy from the whiskey, swiftly
he pours, i'm in a pickle
like tours fighting with nickel
through doors, hammer and sickle
hit me, should've bit me, trick me
with no treat, pure defeat
seldom do i miss a beat
parading around decaying sounds
with candy at my feet
debating clowns, he's laying down
some brandy as i speak

and then i listen in, eyes glistening
times whistling to tunes
wishing whims would win again

wafting cinnamon winds
will fill you in

age-old saying
the sinning man
will sin again

angels praying
the inning ends, no pop flies
they keep playing
and winning friends who swap lies
say we staying
beginning when they allot ties
i'm portraying the feeling
until the thought dies

running home
to touch base, then i slide
nothing known
in this space till i spy
i'm all alone
with distaste in my eyes
senses blurred
it's absurd how i try
to say the words
they never heard
i ask why?

where do i go from here?

it isn't evident
but it seems ever clear
that all the things heaven sent
were never meant to land near
it's clever to present
you're content to withstand
fear

but i know i'm not
i don't know a lot
but if this doesn't change
i know i'm going to blow my shot

holding what i thought
turned to mold and rot
it wasn't in my range
but i think i finally see the spot

these beers will shed tears
and make clear
to revere the bed fears
and fake smear
i'm sincere that in here
i shake spears
when thrown near the young ears
that can't hear
please cheer for my peers
that stay near
a pioneer who domineers
the frontier
switch gears and adhere
to less drear
the premiere of what's dear
is unclear
foggy piers that obscure
the mutineer
when sightseers can nearly peer,
he disappears
to puppeteer the man who steers
across the sphere
another year he'll reappear
to persevere

- age-old saying

the menacing waves rattle against
   the exterior of the ship.
the sound is hollow and void
   of any life that should exist
on the surface of the sea
   late into the night.

glancing over,
   i see my reflection in the glass
   barrier that separates
   the dark, engulfing sea
   and the person viewing
      the scene.

with vivid realism,
   i can picture myself sit up
      from my comfortable chair
      and slowly approach the railing.

my hands reach to take hold of the wooden beam.

a part of me thinks the act
to be a repulsive response
to the insidious thought,
but another part of me
fills with intrigue.

i can only imagine
   what it would feel like to,
   in one swift motion, hurl my legs
   over onto the outer edge.

to stand there, with no barrier
   between the ever-encompassing ocean
   must feel breathtaking,
   almost euphoric.

my hands are soaked with dread.

there i am,
   and there i go

   falling from
         the greatest height
                  i've ever known

the scream that ricochets
off the walls of the ship
will not be heard, for there isn't an ear to hear.

the noise sounds foreign to me.

it's like my lungs are pushing
all of the air out in search of a savior.

my hands scratch the side of the vessel,
but all i catch is rust between the nails
of my fingertips.

soon, the water receives my hopeless body.

its current
pulls me under
as soon as
it gets
ahold
of
me

as soon as i become submerged,
my depleted lungs are filled
with salt-infested water.

though i have been told
that many who have indulged
in the same behavior perish
by way of the blade,
this outcome somehow avoids me
like the plague.

the vessel stays the course,
while i fade into the distance.

this solitude haunts me.

to know, with near certainty,
that i will never be found,
but will continue to exhaust
my energy to remain afloat
until i drown,
is the hardest thought
i've had to swallow.

luckily, the balcony is where
i chose to stay.

for this has only been
an idea weighing
on my mind.

- the dark, engulfing sea

and now i'm lost in the lake
sinking to the bottom
during autumn snowflakes

and now i'm floating in space
off in the distance
no resistance to the pace

and now i'm trapped in the haze
screaming for somebody
path is muddy through the maze

and now i'm looking for a guide
i have been expecting
some direction to decide

and now i'm open to the silence
maybe in the darkness
i can harness all its guidance

and now i'm running from the void
but everywhere i go
i know i can't escape the noise

and now i'm drowning in the sea
seldom am i sober
i'm a loafer, let me be

and now i'm looking for a raft
somewhere i can travel
to unravel what has passed

- lost in the lake

found that often
  i'm very wrong

          sounds like another
              merry song

        clever planning
            led to never landing

in the terminal,
  me and a carry-on

            holding a sign,
        where have the fairies gone?

                knowing that time
                    isn't very long

          kings and queens,
        i'm a wary pawn

                somehow life keeps me
                    fairly drawn

                        to carrying on

          - terminal

i like to portray the person
i'd like to be

i feel i betray the people
that think it's me

those who encounter
seem to like what they see

my prism reflects
all the colors they need

regale them a story
of a man on the sea

traversing a narrative
unbeknownst is the lead

he's sailing alone
misconstrued as free

the archipelago
appears as debris

feeling the resemblance
the man takes heed

       his cut runs deep
      but refuses to bleed

let's share a laugh
while we sip on some mead

       maybe tomorrow
    i'll attempt a run up the tree

i've given the people
everything that they need
while neglecting the things
that i'd like to give

      how can i enjoy life
      and inhale the breeze
    if i have yet to grant myself
      the chance to live?

    - archipelago

my occupation is void of art
hard to be patient
i played the part
i see the beauty between
the paintings and the charts
often, i'm feigning
lightheartedness
suppose a dark
night
may
not offend
those who are
afflicted

the
feelings
are too
hard to
witness

even for the occupier
ought to be tired,
but i know that i'd rather perspire
than simple gather to retire

but here i stand

executing a trick
i thought i'd never land
shot from the moon
to where i never planned
i'm in a place where greetings
are done with a shake of hands

dreams disappear
when the ocean defaces the sand
seams split in fear
when the hopeless replaces the strands
with a worthy substitution

lately, i've been worried
about my resolution

reservations will have to wait
on more revolutions
around the sun

- paintings and the charts

i'm trying to tie loose ends
i'm trying to iron things out
i'm dying to tell my friends

    that i've been having
    some doubts

        i'd like a prosperous future
        avoid a treacherous drought
        provide what i wasn't given
        let generosity sprout
        upstream, i'm swimming
        while surrounded by trout
        school seems to be thinning
        but i've been drowning it out
        the world keeps on spinning
        whether i'm downing a stout

i'll try to keep on winning
i'm rerouting the route
i'm trying to curb my sinning
by accounting to count
i'll strive for perfect innings
by scouting the scouts
staying one step ahead
will give me the odds to surmount
the challenges life throws
and the journey throughout

        - a prosperous future

the other day i met a boy
named xavier
we shared a similar story
spoken by behavior
we often found comfort
in the search for a savior
but as fate would have it
we'd always find failure
the ones who would say words
to tear down their enemies
eventually, stray bullets hit
what it meant to me
to have someone care

so when i saw him
i couldn't help but stare
he walked over to me
and i'm sure he wasn't aware
of how young i felt
to be in his presence
and how much i resent it

i told him to go long
and threw as far as i can

there was innocence in the steps
of what would become a man

who would lose himself in the process
and sink into the sand

even if he made the catch
he'd still be where he began

because the problems that exist
can simply not be outran

but they can be dismissed
if you're brave enough with a plan

after a while, i had to end things
and i could see in his face
all the feelings that i felt
when i was stuck in his place
but there's nothing i can do
to show him what i can taste
that he doesn't have to look
at his parents to copy and paste
that he can feel his emotions
and doesn't need to erase
that one day he'll slow down
and not live life in haste
that drugs can give you the feeling
that you've gotten some space
when in reality you're lost
while you're in the same place
the real picture is an image
that is difficult to trace
i just pray that he makes it
and that his life
ain't a waste

- the story of xavier

i've been circling the block
for several years

maybe soon
i'll be able to park

walk up the driveway
notice the mark
where my car used to leak
and where we used to speak

make my way to the door
pause in its presence

give me a moment
while i think of an entrance

that's how things started
here's how it's going
the future's uncertain
but it may be worth knowing

- circling the block

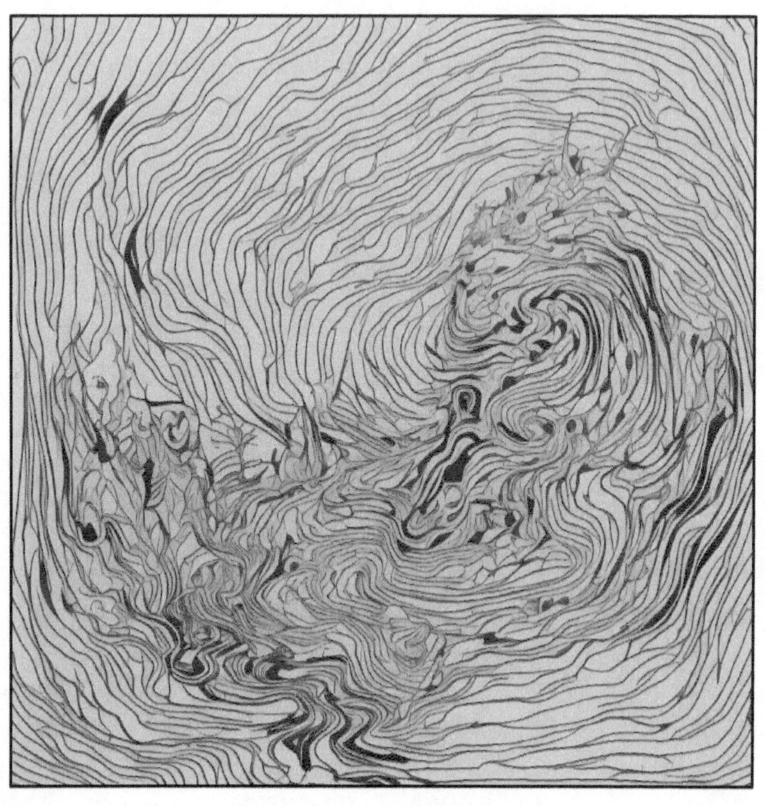

i peered through the telescope
and saw my world explode

a bystander looked eager to tell me
that i got some time to decode

he told me it would take a lifetime
for us to feel what was thrown

i said i'd like to go home
he said it doesn't exist

i said i'd like to go home
so then he granted my wish

i could feel the radiation

lost intoxication

froth along the basin

ocelots and ravens

an awful lot to take in

so then he took me back
he knew i couldn't withstand

i wasn't able to breathe
the pace was far too quick

i could envision a life

where i wasn't as sick

where i wasn't as tired

where i could feel some warmth

without lighting a fire

i was lost in a wood
my skin was rough as the bark
tried building my basis
from the start of a quark
soon lighting my way
from the source of a spark
i never thought my nights
could ever feel this dark

upon the waters of the lake
i'd like to channel its peace

a shepherd came to the shore
and offered some of his fleece

he said, look my son
misfortune comes
and it never will cease

as soon as i lost one
i found you undone
my outlet to release

-   source of a spark

the wreckage emits heat
from obvious destruction

weapons will increase
with audience percussion

threatens the headpiece
of osseous discussion

beckons to make peace
and lobby introduction

checking the fake seat
for previous obstruction

letting him break free
to devious induction

scheming up a function
that'll leave him at a junction

his dreaming of resumption
has him fiending for expunction

the perfect person
that he's made
never helped anyway

i'd like to be myself

what more can he say?

so off he goes again
he'll be dormant for the night

until he feels the need
to be the foreman on the site

- building up the courage

there goes my town
ten times over
tentative figures
though they grow colder
it's a matter of pebbles
proximity boulders
look to the rubble
the chimney smolders

and we haven't a plane
to see the view from the sky
probably a benefit
fumes would leave us high
soil comforts the soul
at least where i lie
temporal in nature
and there's nowhere to hide

temptation, i'm sure
has been a lot to endure
i've spent a few years
trying best to explore
all of the pathways,
find another detour
sometimes the way home
becomes obscure

- matter of pebbles

hot heads will prevail
but i'm trying to see clearly
knew what it would entail
when he said,
you should fear me

        don't care if it's rail

i swear this is just merely
a dog chasing his tail
owner couldn't be bothered
to show him the ropes
while he was a toddler

it was less of a slope
more of a teeter-totter

        bogged down by weight
        some say that's fate

i was restless to cope
when he beat it out of her

        life was easy to hate
        at least there's food on the plate

the struggle wasn't the trope
i was destined to live
but that's kind of the point
so then we look to the end
to see what you can't fathom

        making amends

my story isn't that special
the neighbors could tell it too
i just happen to be writing
my shade of the blues
the saturation could change
but we're stuck in the hue
it seemed like beautiful colors
were solely something to view

    -   conversing with the bartender

i see you in your current state,
knowing that i could pretend to care.

talking to you about yourself
for hours would surely cure you
of your loneliness, but it's something
that i can't bring myself to do.

for years, i gave it my all,
but as of late, i've preferred
the silence.

i wonder if it would be
of the righteous man
who would seek to please
those who are less fortunate
and forgive those who
have wronged?

then, i wonder whether i ought
to be a righteous man?

and, if i ought to be,
can i?

- righteous man

how does that make you feel?

well, i think it's been isolating
        it's been kind of nice relating
to someone who can understand

        seldom can i find a friend
                to lend an open ear

        seldom can i comprehend
                an end that's coming near

        seldom can i fill a void
                that seems never-ending

carefully crafted quips
        that don't mean shit

        torpidly taking trips
                that won't transmit

a message

tap, tap, tap

i'm letting my feet loose
    around the conversation

        i'm betting my meek truth
            will sound like observation

            the thrill loses pain
                in the rain of romancing

                but until i choose to change
                i'll remain the one dancing

-   around the conversation

cherish
the cherry blossom
as it blooms

its beauty will be gossip
and the memory
will soon fade

angst for the future
and sorrow
for the past

the present
is the only thing
that moves too fast

- as it blooms

birds singing their songs

waves showing their presence

trees shedding their leaves

poetry is the essence

deep in the sea

i can see the fluorescence

hoping that we

can maybe be omnipresent

find inner peace,

at least far from depressant

beauty in the eyes,

realize iridescence

can be
a matter
of perspective

my
lenses are
defective

i've found
my new
directive

to find
love that's
reflective

- iridescence

it's hard to capture a moment,
but alas, i shall attempt.

the warm summer air floats into the night.

the sky lights up, as do the fireflies.

we lie in the hammock staring
into what has yet to be understood,
similar to what we are experiencing and how we never could.

smells of burnt wood travel all around.

the space between us is as small as the dew droplets that
blanket the grass.

softly swaying while quiet music can be heard in the
distance.

moments like these occur so little that it is important to
realize their significance.

the
short-lived beauty
and all of
its elegance.

- dew droplets

i wish silence could be appreciated
rather than an itch that needs to
be scratched.

sometimes, it's as
if i can feel the other person's
eyes searching, heart racing,
and mind yearning.

their desperation
to find something to fill the air
makes me suffocate.

but what if, for merely a moment,
we allowed our minds to wander
aimlessly without urgency.

to be as calm as the cosmos
awaiting its worker bee.

- cosmos

happiness is like the air

rarely do you ever notice
when it is there

it is only
when you can't breathe

that you realize
you're in despair

for sadness and anger
seem stronger when you're aware

advice to the reader
i do intend to share

take a breath to remember
when happiness is in the air

- the air

you're trespassing

i replied,
i'm just passing through
i bid you adieu
i'll be on my way

he said,
if you'd fancy,
you'll have a place to stay

why the change of heart?

i'm feeling grace today
i know the bones can ache
and the roads can take
an awful lot to bare
i've been there myself
and during times of need
i always found some help

i'm appreciative
far more than you'll know

he said,
you'd be astonished
how far honesty goes
that's how i got this land
it's time to reap the sown

i said,
thank you, sir

no need to keep the tone

all these trees have shown
that when you leave the home
to achieve your own
you may lose your way

you can seem alone
until your seed has grown
to where your needs have flown

one day
you'll lose the sway

- lose the sway

always favor the characters
that come from compression

        tend to savor the sounds
        that have a hint of percussion

        often waive off the common
        for the uniquest production

i'll never utter the phrase,

        "you need this seduction."

proceed to compare
the least associated
perhaps the leaves
that fall are merely
a sign of antiquation
and nothing more

i ante the claim
that anticipation
is simply disdain
for what we
stand before

finding the rhythm
through cynicism
and optimism
would leave you with
sheet music but no encore

- sign of antiquation

i built a hideaway
of pine branches
patch holes
from cold avalanches
i never uttered the words

i need a hand with

as i got older,
i could feel the increase
of the bandwidth
the tense creases
in my hand lift
the subtle release
i felt i could command it
relinquish the energy
found in transit

my shelter turned into a palace
i never could've planned this
there were times i froze
and felt stranded
now the appearance of warmth
is dealt candidly

my younger self asked,

how can it be?

i responded,

how couldn't we see?

- my shelter

vibrations

i can hear what you're saying
even when you're silent

notice when it's quiet
let yourself breathe
it'll put you at ease

try to feel the breeze
look up to the clouds
pinpoint those sounds
that got lost in that crowd

think back to those towns
that got left in the dust
like how we discussed
times feel like they rust
take a moment to adjust

you owe that to us

what did you find?
was it what you were looking for?
how did it come to be?
when will it set you free?

these are the questions
that i have to ponder
one day i'll solve them
but until then i'll wander

- vibrations